MO VAUGHN

BIG MO

By Andrew Santella

Children's Press®
A Division of Grolier Publishing
New York London Hong Kong Sydney
Danbury, Connecticut

Photo Credits

Cover, Focus on Sports; 5, ©Rob Tringali, Jr./SportsChrome East/West;
6, SportsChrome East/West; 9, Janet Knott/*The Boston Globe*; 10, ©Damian
Strohmeyer/AllSport; 13, ©Jim Commentucci/AllSport; 14, 15, 16, Courtesy
Trinity-Pawling Prep School, Pawling, NY; 19, ©S. R. Smith; 20, ©Jim
Commentucci/AllSport; 23, ©Michael Zito/SportsChrome East/West; 24,
©Damian Strohmeyer/AllSport; 27, SportsChrome East/West; 29, (top left),
AP/Wide World; 29 (top right and bottom), UPI/Bettmann; 30, ©Jonathan
Daniel/AllSport; 33, SportsChrome East/West; 34, AP/Wide World; 36, ©Jim
Bourg/Reuters/Archive Photos; 37, 39, AP/Wide World; 40, ©Matt West/*Boston
Herald*; 43, ©Jim Commentucci/AllSport; 44 (left), Courtesy Trinity-Pawling
Prep School, Pawling, NY; 44 (right), ©Michael Zito/SportsChrome East/West;
45 (left), ©Damian Strohmeyer/AllSport; 45 (right), ©Jim Commentucci/
AllSport; 46, ©Otto Greule/AllSport; 47, SportsChrome East/West

Editorial Staff

Project Editor: Mark Friedman
Design: Herman Adler Design Group
Photo Editor: Jan Izzo

Library of Congress Cataloging-in-Publication Data

Santella, Andrew.
    Mo Vaughn : Big Mo / by Andrew Santella.
      p. cm. – (Sports stars)
    Summary: Describes the private life and baseball career of the man
named Most Valuable Player for the Boston Red Sox in both 1993 and 1994.
    ISBN 0-516-04369-2
    1. Vaughn, Mo—Juvenile literature. 2. Baseball players—United
States—Biography—Juvenile literature. 3. Boston Red Sox (Baseball
team)—Juvenile literature. [1. Vaughn, Mo. 2. Baseball players. 3. Afro-
Americans—Biography.] I. Title. II. Series.
GV865.V38S25   1996
796.357'092–dc20   95-47756
[B]   CIP
                                      AC

MO VAUGHN
BIG MO

Red Sox fans call him "Big Mo." It's a fitting nickname for Maurice (Mo) Vaughn, the slugging first baseman for the Boston Red Sox. He stands six-foot-one and weighs 245 pounds. When he steps to the plate, he carries a 36-inch, 36-ounce bat. And when he cuts loose with one of his giant swings, he can make baseballs fly as far as any hitter in the game.

Big Mo is one of the biggest stars to hit Boston in years. But he is popular not only for his big swing. He also has a big heart. Mo Vaughn produces on the baseball field, but he finds time to make people happy off the field, too.

In 1995, Mo won the American League's Most
Valuable Player award. It was yet another big
reward for his work in a baseball uniform. Out
of uniform, Mo has done even more good work for
his community. In 1994, he opened a youth center
in Mattapan, a tough neighborhood in Boston. Mo
wanted to build a place where kids could improve
their reading skills and receive career counseling.
That's how Mo lives — the more successful he is
on the field, the more good he does off the field.

Mo often talks to groups of schoolchildren.
He urges them to stay in school. He signs get-well
cards and visits sick people in hospitals. He uses
money he earns from signing his autograph to
pay for poor kids to go to the circus. These are
some of Mo's many good deeds that make him
stand so tall.

Mo Vaughn spends a lot of time with children. He urges them to stay in school and complete their education.

Pitchers fear the task of facing Mo Vaughn.

Mo Vaughn grew up in Norwalk, Connecticut, which is not far from New York City. Playing Little League baseball there, Mo quickly developed into a great hitter. When he was 11 years old, he hit a home run that flew about 350 feet. It would have gone even farther if it hadn't hit a building! People in Norwalk still say it was the longest home run a Little Leaguer has ever hit there.

Opposing pitchers learned not to pitch to him. If he came to the plate with the bases loaded, the other team usually walked him intentionally. They figured it was better to walk a run in than to let Mo hit a grand slam.

Mo always had fun playing baseball. His Little League coaches remember him smiling all the time, even while trying his best to win. When Mo took batting practice, he always wanted his coaches to throw harder and harder. Then he would wallop a pitch over the fence, smile, and ask for an even faster pitch.

Mo spent many hours working on his batting skills. He seemed always to be playing ball at a high-school field near his home. His first coaches were his parents. In fact, Mo's mother was his first batting coach. When Mo was two years old and his father was working, his mother took Mo out to the yard for hitting lessons. Even though Mo was a natural right-hander, his mother taught him to hit left-handed. Everyone in her family was left-handed, so she taught Mo that way. Mo has been a left-handed hitter ever since.

In high school, Mo worked hard in class (above), and he became a star in many sports, including basketball (facing page, sixth from right.)

Mo was less enthusiastic about school than he was about baseball. But Mo's parents were teachers. His mother, Shirley, taught first grade in Norwalk for 30 years. His father was a junior-high and high-school principal there. So they would not let Mo's grades suffer while he devoted all his energy to sports. When he was 15, Mo's parents felt he needed more school discipline. So they sent him to a boarding school called Trinity Pawling Prep in Pawling, New York.

Mo takes a break during a high-school football game.

Moving away from home was a big adjustment. Mo quickly learned about taking responsibility for himself and getting along with others. He grew more dedicated to his schoolwork, and he still found time to play a lot of baseball, basketball, and football. In the summers, he played on traveling baseball teams made up of the best high-school athletes in the area. He faced pitchers who were being scouted by big colleges and major-league baseball teams.

At the same time, Mo was becoming "Big Mo." As a teen, he developed the muscular physique he is famous for today. And the stronger he got, the harder he hit. And the harder he hit, the more people noticed him. As pro scouts began watching him, Mo started thinking he might be able to make it as a major-league baseball player.

By the time Mo graduated from Trinity Pawling in 1986, he was known to every baseball scout in the East. The Philadelphia Phillies selected Mo in the fifth round of baseball's amateur draft. But Mo chose not to sign a contract with Philadelphia. He listened to the good advice of his parents. A few more years of growth would be good before he entered the high-pressure world of pro baseball.

Mo enrolled at Seton Hall University in South Orange, New Jersey. He was happy there because he was close to his family in Norwalk. In fact, his parents, siblings, and friends often came to Seton Hall to watch him play college baseball.

Mo playing first base for Seton Hall University

Mo made an impact right away. In his freshman year, he hit 28 home runs, the most by any freshman in Seton Hall history. One of those home runs was a tremendous 500-foot shot. Just as in Little League, people could not believe how hard and how far Mo could hit the ball.

During the summer, Mo played in the Cape Cod League for college players. As always, his family was there for support. His parents stayed with nearby relatives so they could be near their son. They even pitched batting practice to Mo, just as they did when he was a kid. Even today, Mo's parents love to watch him play. They are now retired and live in Virginia, but they fly to Boston whenever the Red Sox play home games. They also travel to eastern cities such as Toronto or Baltimore to cheer him on. And when they can't be together, they speak on the phone.

Mo Vaughn was named an All-American
player in each of his three seasons at Seton Hall.
His batting average was .417, and he set school
records with 57 home runs and 218 runs batted
in. He was named the school league's player of
the decade. After Mo graduated from college
with a degree in communications, he decided
it was time to play in the majors.

In 1989, the Boston Red Sox selected Mo
in the first round of the draft. He was the 23rd
player picked overall. But as great a college star
as he was, Mo was not ready for the big leagues.
Like most players, Mo had to prove himself
in the minor leagues. His first stop was New
Britain, Connecticut, home of the Red Sox
AA minor-league team. The next year, he was
promoted to AAA and played at Pawtucket,
Rhode Island.

The Boston Red Sox claimed Mo in the 1989 amateur draft.

Ever since childhood, Mo has remained close to his mother. Here, they attend a Boston charity event together.

Mo started slowly in AAA ball. He hit just .186 in April, and then his hand was broken when it was hit by a pitch. After his injury healed, he continued to struggle at the plate. Some young players would have panicked in such a slump. But Mo and his family responded in typical fashion. Mo's mother loaded her car with a pitching machine that she and Mo practiced with years before. She drove 150 miles to Pawtucket, and the next day, she fed him dozens of practice pitches. Mo took swing after swing as his mother chased down balls in the outfield.

Batting practice with Mom made the difference. Mo quickly came out of his slump. In the last 82 games of the season, Mo hit .338 with 17 home runs. He was named his team's most valuable player for the season. And in 1991, he kept on hitting. In 39 games, he hit 13 home runs. One was a rarity: a broken-bat homer. The ball sailed over the fence while Mo was left holding nothing but the handle of his broken bat!

By June 1991, the Red Sox were convinced. Mo was called up to the major leagues.

Mo hit his first major-league home run
in Baltimore in just his fourth game. It was
no ordinary homer. It sailed 438 feet and just
missed flying completely out of the stadium.
The next night, he drove in four runs. In his
first 12 games, he hit .318 with three homers.

It was an amazing start, and he had Boston
fans buzzing. They compared him to great
Red Sox sluggers of the past — Jim Rice, Carl
Yastrzemski, even Ted Williams. Even when
he hit a slump, Boston fans still loved their
new hero. His positive attitude and hard
work earned him praise.

Mo follows in a long line of outstanding Boston sluggers, including Ted Williams (top right), Carl Yastrzemski (bottom), and Jim Rice (top left).

The 1992 season began with a big slump
for Big Mo. It got so bad that he went 19 at
bats without a hit. The Red Sox had not lost
confidence in him, but they sent him to
Pawtucket so he could work on his hitting.
It was Mo's last trip to the minors. When he
came back to Boston, he established himself
as a clutch hitter late in the game. In fact,
he hit .302 in the last three innings of games.
These are the at bats with the most pressure,
when the game is on the line.

Mo also did what he always does when he struggles. He worked harder and harder to improve. The Red Sox hired a new hitting coach, Mike Easler, in 1993. Mo was one of Easler's first projects. They worked long hours on his swing, his stance, and his confidence. The work paid off.

Mo broke through to stardom in 1993. He had no major slumps, and he hit spectacularly in the clutch. His 29 home runs and 101 runs batted in were the best power numbers by a Red Sox player in five years. He was named team MVP, and even drew some votes for MVP in the American League.

In 1993, Mo worked with hitting coach Mike Easler and improved his swing.

NORFOLK PUBLIC SCHOOLS
NORFOLK, MA 02056

Mo gets a high-five after slugging a home run.

In 1994, Mo proved he was no fluke. Even though he was bothered by injuries, he hit .310. Like the pitchers in the Little League, big-league pitchers began avoiding Mo when men were on base. They intentionally walked him more than any other hitter in the league.

But as good as Mo was, the rest of the Red Sox were not a very good team. The 1994 season was disastrous for Boston, as well as for the entire sport of baseball. As the sport was torn apart by a players' strike that canceled the World Series, the Red Sox struggled through their third straight losing season. Their ace pitcher, Roger Clemens, was injured and his career was in doubt. Several other players were getting older, struggling with injuries, or suffering through slumps.

When the baseball strike ended in April 1995, not many people expected big things from the Red Sox. But new players joined the team, and Boston surprised everyone by running away with the American League Eastern Division title. Slugger Jose Canseco, rookie Troy O'Leary, and shortstop John Valentin (Mo's teammate at Seton Hall) joined Mo to form a potent Boston lineup.

After clinching the American League East in 1995, Mo jumped on a police horse to lead Boston fans' cheers.

At the 1995 All-Star Game, Mo jokes with Ken Griffey, Jr. (center), and Tino Martinez (left).

In the post-season, Mo Vaughn and the Red Sox were not strong enough to overcome the unbeatable Cleveland Indians. The Indians eliminated the Red Sox in the first round of the playoffs, and they went on to win the American League pennant.

In November 1995, however, Mo achieved
a small victory over Cleveland. When the
American League Most Valuable Player voting
was announced, Mo finished on top. In a tight
race, he defeated Cleveland slugger Albert Belle.
Some baseball fans were surprised. Albert Belle
had better statistics than Mo in most categories.
But Mo had proven himself to be a good citizen
on the field, in the clubhouse, and in his
community. Many baseball reporters voted
for him because of the leadership he provided
for his team.

The Red Sox congratulate their MVP on another 1995 home run.

Mo with one of his many young fans at the Charles Taylor Elementary School.

———————————— ★ ★ ★ ————————————

When the MVP award was announced, Mo
held a press conference at a youth center he
had founded. He said, "I guess it really does say
something. People are looking at the whole thing
and that it's not just numbers. It's important to
have character."

Ever since he became a star, people
throughout New England have known him as
a caring and charitable person. He has used
his fame and wealth to help people in need in
Boston. He established the Mo Vaughn Youth
Center. He makes visits to the Charles Taylor
Elementary School as part of the Red Sox
Adopt-a-School program. And he rarely passes
an opportunity to talk to young people. He tells
kids to stay in school and stay off the streets. ·
Even kids who never talk to Mo learn from him.

Mo Vaughn's fame has grown far beyond Boston. Throughout Massachusetts, Connecticut, and all of New England, kids and adults love Big Mo. He is widely recognized as the most popular athlete in the region since the great Ted Williams. Red Sox fans have seen him improve as a hitter every year. They have witnessed hard work paying off with great success. This is a lesson that Mo learned very early — in Little League, at prep school, and practicing with his family. Now Mo wants to pass those lessons on to others.

C ★ H ★ R ★ O ★ N

1967 • Maurice Vaughn is born on December 15, in
Norwalk, Connecticut.

1982 • Mo enrolls at Trinity Pawling Prep School.

1986 • Mo is drafted by the Philadelphia Phillies, but he
turns them down to attend Seton Hall University.

1987 • Mo sets Seton Hall record with 28 home runs in
one season.

1989 • Mo is drafted by and signs with the Boston Red Sox.
He is named Big East Conference Player of the
Decade for his career at Seton Hall University.

O ⋆ L ⋆ O ⋆ G ⋆ Y

1990 • Playing for Boston's AAA minor-league team at Pawtucket, Rhode Island, Mo hits .295 with 22 home runs. He is named the team's MVP.

1991 • Mo makes his major-league debut with the Boston Red Sox.

1993 • Mo is named MVP of the Red Sox as he hits 29 home runs and collects 101 RBI.

1995 • Mo sets career highs in home runs (36), RBI (126), runs (98), and stolen bases (11). He leads the Red Sox to the American League Eastern Division title and wins the American League MVP award.

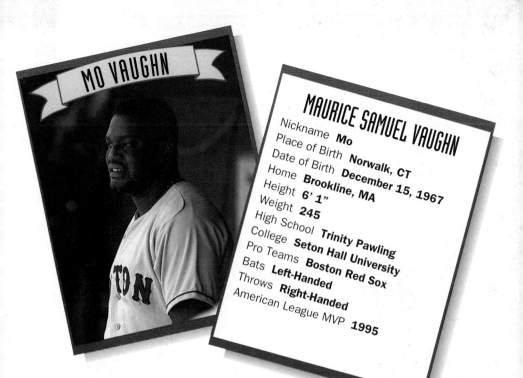

MO VAUGHN

MAURICE SAMUEL VAUGHN

Nickname **Mo**
Place of Birth **Norwalk, CT**
Date of Birth **December 15, 1967**
Home **Brookline, MA**
Height **6' 1"**
Weight **245**
High School **Trinity Pawling**
College **Seton Hall University**
Pro Teams **Boston Red Sox**
Bats **Left-Handed**
Throws **Right-Handed**
American League MVP **1995**

MAJOR-LEAGUE STATISTICS

Season	Team	Batting Average	Home Runs	Runs	Runs Batted In
1991	Boston	.260	4	21	32
1992	Boston	.234	13	42	57
1993	Boston	.297	29	86	101
1994*	Boston	.310	26	65	82
1995	Boston	.300	39	98	126
Total (5 seasons)		**.285**	**111**	**312**	**398**

*1994 season shortened by players' strike

--- ★ ★ ★ ---

About the Author

Andrew Santella is a lifelong resident of Chicago. He is a graduate of Chicago's Loyola University, where he studied American Literature. He writes about history, sports, and popular culture for several magazines for young people, including *Nickelodian Magazine*. For Children's Press, he is the author of *The Capitol*.